Vegetarian Cookbook

The best beginner's guide delicious recipes
for lunch and dinners

Matt Alemu

Table of Contents

1. Baked Shitake Mushrooms and Kohlrabi

1 pound kohlrabi, halved 2 tablespoons extra virgin olive oil 1/2 pound shitake mushrooms 8 cloves unpeeled garlic 3 tablespoons sesame oil sea salt and ground black pepper to taste 1/4 pound cherry tomatoes 3 tablespoons toasted cashew nuts 1/4 pound spinach, thinly sliced

Spread the potatoes in a pan Drizzle with 2 tablespoons of oil and Preheat your oven to 425 degrees F. roast for 15 minutes turning once. Add the mushrooms with the stem sides up Add the garlic cloves to pan and cook until lightly browned Drizzle with 1 tablespoon sesame oil and season with sea salt and black pepper. Return to the oven and bake for 5 min. Add the cherry tomatoes to the pan. Return to oven and bake until mushrooms become softened, for 5 min. Sprinkle the cashew nuts over the kohlrabi and mushrooms. Serve with the spinach.

Notes:

2. Baked Button Mushroom and Summer Squash

1 pound summer squash, halved 2 tablespoons extra virgin olive oil 1/2 pound button mushrooms 8 cloves unpeeled garlic 2 tsp. cumin 1 tsp. annatto seed ½ tsp. cayenne pepper 1 tablespoon extra-virgin olive oil sea salt and ground black pepper to taste 1/4 pound cherry tomatoes 3 tablespoons toasted pine nuts 1/4 pound spinach, thinly sliced

Preheat your oven to 425 degrees F. Spread the summer squash in a pan Drizzle with 2 tablespoons of olive oil and roast for 15 minutes turning once. Add the mushrooms with the stem sides up Add the garlic cloves to pan and cook until lightly browned Sprinkle with cumin , cayenne pepper and annatto seeds. Drizzle with 1 tablespoon olive oil and season with sea salt and black pepper. Return to the oven and bake for 5 min. Add the cherry tomatoes to the pan. Return to oven and bake until mushrooms become softened, for 5 min. Sprinkle the pine nuts over the summer squash and mushrooms. Serve with the spinach.

Notes:

3. Baked Spinach and Butternut Squash

1 ½ pounds butternut squash, peeled and cut into 1-inch chunks ½ red onion, thinly sliced ¼ cup water ½ vegetable stock cube, crumbled 1 tbsp. extra virgin olive oil ½ tsp cumin ½ tsp annatto seeds ½ tsp cayenne pepper ½ tsp hot chili powder Black pepper ½ pound fresh spinach, roughly chopped

DIRECTIONS (20 minutes)

Put all of the ingredients in a slow cooker except the last one. Top with handfuls of spinach and stuff the slow cooker with it. If you can't fit it all in at once, let the first batch cook first and add some more spinach. Cook for 3or 4 hours on medium until squash become soft. Scrape the sides and serve.

Notes:

4. Baked Watercress and Summer Squash

1 ½ pounds summer squash, peeled and cut into 1-inch chunks ½ red onion, thinly sliced ¼ cup water ½ vegetable stock cube, crumbled 1 tbsp. sesame oil ½ tsp Chinese 5 spice powder ½ tsp Sichuan Peppercorns ½ tsp hot chili powder Black pepper ½ pound fresh watercress, roughly chopped

DIRECTIONS (20 minutes)

Put all of the ingredients in a slow cooker except the last one. Top with handfuls of watercress and stuff the slow cooker with it. If you can't fit it all in at once, let the first batch cook first and add some more watercress. Cook for 3 or 4 hours on medium until summer squash become soft. Scrape the sides and serve.

Notes:

5. Curried Kale and Rutabaga

1 ½ pounds Rutabaga, peeled and cut into 1-inch chunks ½ onion, thinly sliced ¼ cup water ½ vegetable stock cube, crumbled 1 tbsp. extra virgin olive oil ½ tsp cumin ½ tsp ground coriander ½ tsp garam masala ½ tsp hot chili powder Black pepper ½ pound fresh kale, roughly chopped

DIRECTIONS (20 minutes)

Put all of the ingredients in a slow cooker except the last one. Top with handfuls of kale and stuff the slow cooker with it. If you can't fit it all in at once, let the first batch cook first and add some more kale. Cook for 3or 4 hours on medium until root vegetables become soft. Scrape the sides and serve

Notes:

6. Buttered Potatoes and Spinach

1 ½ pounds red potatoes, peeled and cut into 1-inch chunks ½ onion, thinly sliced ¼ cup water ½ vegetable stock cube, crumbled 2 tbsp. salted butter ½ tsp herbs de Provence ½ tsp thyme ½ tsp hot chili powder Black pepper ½ pound fresh spinach, roughly chopped

DIRECTIONS (20 minutes)

Put all of the ingredients in a slow cooker except the last one. Top with handfuls of spinach and stuff the slow cooker with it. If you can't fit it all in at once, let the first batch cook first and add some more spinach. Cook for 3or 4 hours on medium until potatoes become soft. Scrape the sides and serve.

Notes:

7. Roasted Vegan-Buttered Mustard Greens Carrots

1 ½ pounds carrots, peeled and cut into 1-inch chunks ½ onion, thinly sliced ¼ cup water ½ vegetable stock cube, crumbled 1 tbsp. butter 1 tsp garlic, minced ½ tsp lemon juice Black pepper ½ pound fresh mustard greens, roughly chopped

DIRECTIONS (20 minutes)

Put all of the ingredients in a slow cooker except the last one. Top with handfuls of mustard greens and stuff the slow cooker with it. If you can't fit it all in at once, let the first batch cook first and add some more mustard greens. Cook for 3or 4 hours on medium until carrots become soft. Scrape the sides and serve.

Notes:

8. Smoky Roasted Swiss Chard and Cauliflower

1 ½ pounds cauliflower, peeled and cut into 1-inch chunks ½ red onion, thinly sliced ¼ cup water ½ vegetable stock cube, crumbled 1 tbsp. extra virgin olive oil ½ tsp cumin ½ tsp hot chili powder Black pepper ½ pound fresh Swiss chard, roughly chopped

DIRECTIONS (20 minutes)

Put all of the ingredients in a slow cooker except the last one. Top with handfuls of Swiss chard and stuff the slow cooker with it. If you can't fit it all in at once, let the first batch cook first and add some more Swiss chard. Cook for 3or 4 hours on medium until potatoes become soft. Scrape the sides and serve.

Notes:

9. Roasted Microgreens and Potatoes

1 ½ pounds potatoes, peeled and cut into 1-inch chunks ½ onion, thinly sliced ¼ cup water ½ vegetable stock cube, crumbled 1 tbsp. olive oil ½ tsp minced ginger 2 sprigs lemon grass ½ tsp green onions, minced ½ tsp hot chili powder Black pepper ½ pound Microgreens, roughly chopped

DIRECTIONS (20 minutes)

Put all of the ingredients in a slow cooker except the last one. Top with handfuls of Microgreens and stuff the slow cooker with it. If you can't fit it all in at once, let the first batch cook first and add some more Microgreens. Cook for 3or 4 hours on medium until potatoes become soft. Scrape the sides and serve.

Notes:

10. Roasted Spinach & Broccoli with Jalapeno

1 ½ pounds broccoli florets ½ onion, thinly sliced ¼ cup water ½ vegetable stock cube, crumbled 1 tbsp. extra virgin olive oil ½ tsp cumin 8 jalapeno peppers, finely chopped 1 ancho chili ½ tsp hot chili powder Black pepper ½ pound fresh spinach, roughly chopped

DIRECTIONS (20 minutes)

Put all of the ingredients in a slow cooker except the last one. Top with handfuls of spinach and stuff the slow cooker with it. If you can't fit it all in at once, let the first batch cook first and add some more spinach. Cook for 3or 4 hours on medium until broccoli become soft. Scrape the sides and serve.

Notes:

11. Spicy Baked Swiss Chard and Cauliflower

1 ½ pounds cauliflower florets, blanched (dipped in boiling water then dipped in ice water) ½ cup bean sprouts, rinsed ½ cup water ½ vegetable stock cube, crumbled 1 tbsp. sesame oil ½ tsp Thai chili paste ½ tsp Sriracha hot sauce ½ tsp hot chili powder 2 Thai bird chilies, minced Black pepper ½ pound fresh Swiss chard, roughly chopped

Put all of the ingredients in a slow cooker except the last one. Top with handfuls of Swiss chard and stuff the slow cooker with it. If you can't fit it all in at once, let the first batch cook first and add some more Swiss chard. Cook for 3 or 4 hours on medium until potatoes become soft. Scrape the sides and serve.

Notes:

12. Thai Carrots and Collard Greens

1 ½ pounds carrots, peeled and cut into 1-inch chunks ½ onion, thinly sliced ¼ cup water ½ vegetable stock cube, crumbled 1 tbsp. extra virgin olive oil 1 tbsp. sesame oil ½ tsp Thai chili paste ½ tsp Sriracha hot sauce ½ tsp hot chili powder 2 Thai bird chilies, minced Black pepper ½ pound collard greens, roughly chopped

DIRECTIONS (20 minutes)

Put all of the ingredients in a slow cooker except the last one. Top with handfuls of collard greens and stuff the slow cooker with it. If you can't fit it all in at once, let the first batch cook first and add some more collard greens. Cook for 3or 4 hours on medium until carrots become soft. Scrape the sides and serve.

Notes:

13. Baked White Yam and Spinach

½ pounds potatoes, peeled and cut into 1-inch chunks ½ pounds white yam, peeled and cut into 1-inch chunks ½ pounds carrots, peeled and cut into 1-inch chunks ½ red onion, thinly sliced ¼ cup water ½ vegetable stock cube, crumbled 1 tbsp. extra virgin olive oil ½ tsp cumin ½ tsp ground coriander ½ tsp garam masala ½ tsp cayenne pepper Black pepper ½ pound fresh spinach, roughly chopped

DIRECTIONS (20 minutes)

Put all of the ingredients in a slow cooker except the last one. Top with handfuls of spinach and stuff the slow cooker with it. If you can't fit it all in at once, let the first batch cook first and add some more spinach. Cook for 3or 4 hours on medium until potatoes become soft. Scrape the sides and serve.

Notes:

14. Southeast Asian Baked Turnip Greens & Carrots

INGREDIENTS (4 Servings)

½ pound turnips, peeled and cut into 1-inch chunks ½ pound carrots, peeled and cut into 1-inch chunks ½ pound parsnips, peeled and cut into 1-inch chunks ½ red onion, thinly sliced ½ cup vegetable broth 1 tbsp. extra virgin olive oil ½ tsp minced ginger 2 stalks lemon grass 8 cloves garlic, minced Black pepper ½ pound fresh turnip greens, roughly chopped

DIRECTIONS (20 minutes)

Put all of the ingredients in a slow cooker except the last one. Top with handfuls of turnip greens and stuff the slow cooker with it. If you can't fit it all in at once, let the first batch cook first and add some more turnip greens. Cook for 3or 4 hours on medium until turnips become soft. Scrape the sides and serve.

Notes:

15. Curried Watercress and Potatoes

1 ½ pounds potatoes, peeled and cut into 1-inch chunks ½ onion, thinly sliced ¼ cup water ½ vegetable stock cube, crumbled 1 tbsp. extra virgin olive oil ½ tsp cumin ½ tsp ground coriander ½ tsp garam masala ½ tsp hot chili powder Black pepper ½ pound fresh Watercress, roughly chopped

DIRECTIONS (20 minutes)

Put all of the ingredients in a slow cooker except the last one. Top with handfuls of watercress and stuff the slow cooker with it. If you can't fit it all in at once, let the first batch cook first and add some more watercress. Cook for 3or 4 hours on medium until potatoes become soft. Scrape the sides and serve.

Notes:

16. Jalapeno Kale and Parsnips

1 ½ pounds parsnips, peeled and cut into 1-inch chunks ½ red onion, thinly sliced ¼ cup water ½ vegetable stock cube, crumbled 1 tbsp. extra virgin olive oil ½ tsp cumin ½ tsp jalapeno pepper, minced 1 ancho chili, minced Black pepper ½ pound Kale, roughly chopped

DIRECTIONS (20 minutes)

Put all of the ingredients in a slow cooker except the last one. Top with handfuls of kale and stuff the slow cooker with it. If you can't fit it all in at once, let the first batch cook first and add some more Kale. Cook for 3or 4 hours on medium until parsnips become soft. Scrape the sides and serve.

Notes:

17. Spicy Choy Sum and Broccoli

INGREDIENTS (4 Servings)

1 pound broccoli, peeled and cut into 1-inch chunks ½ pound button mushrooms, sliced ½ onion, thinly sliced ¼ cup water ½ vegetable stock cube, crumbled 1 tbsp. sesame oil ½ tsp Chinese five spice powder ½ tsp Sichuan peppercorns ½ tsp hot chili powder Black pepper ½ pound choy sum, roughly chopped

DIRECTIONS (20 minutes)

Put all of the ingredients in a slow cooker except the last one. Top with handfuls of choy sum and stuff the slow cooker with it. If you can't fit it all in at once, let the first batch cook first and add some more choy sum. Cook for 3or 4 hours on medium until broccoli become soft. Scrape the sides and serve.

Notes:

18. Kale and Potatoes in Pesto Sauce

INGREDIENTS (4 Servings)

1 ½ pounds potatoes, peeled and cut into 1-inch chunks ½ onion, thinly sliced ¼ cup vegetable stock 1 tbsp. extra virgin olive oil 2 tbsp. pesto sauce Black pepper ½ pound fresh Kale, roughly chopped

DIRECTIONS (20 minutes)

Put all of the ingredients in a slow cooker except the last one. Top with handfuls of Kale and stuff the slow cooker with it. If you can't fit it all in at once, let the first batch cook first and add some more Kale. Cook for 3 or 4 hours on medium until potatoes become soft. Scrape the sides and serve.

Notes:

19. Turnip Greens and Kohlrabi in Pesto Sauce

1 ½ pounds kohlrabi,peeled and cut into 1-inch chunks ½ onion, thinly sliced ¼ cup vegetable stock 1 tbsp. extra virgin olive oil 2 tbsp. pesto sauce Black pepper ½ pound fresh Turnip Greens, roughly chopped

DIRECTIONS (20 minutes)

Put all of the ingredients in a slow cooker except the last one. Top with handfuls of Turnip Greens and stuff the slow cooker with it. If you can't fit it all in at once, let the first batch cook first and add some more Turnip Greens. Cook for 3or 4 hours on medium until kohlrabi become soft. Scrape the sides and serve.

Notes:

20. Bok Choy and Kohlrabi in Chili Garlic Sauce

1 ½ pounds kohlrabi, peeled and cut into 1-inch chunks ½ onion, thinly sliced ¼ cup vegetable stock 1 tbsp. sesame oil 4 cloves garlic, minced 2 tbsp. chili garlic sauce Black pepper ½ pound fresh Bok Choy, roughly chopped

Put all of the ingredients in a slow cooker except the last one. Top with handfuls of Bok Choy and stuff the slow cooker with it. If you can't fit it all in at once, let the first batch cook first and add some more Bok Choy. Cook for 3 or 4 hours on medium until kohlrabi become soft. Scrape the sides and serve.

Notes:

21. Slow Cooked Kale and Summer Squash

1 ½ pounds summer squash, peeled and cut into 1-inch chunks ½ onion, thinly sliced ¼ cup vegetable stock 1 tbsp. extra virgin olive oil 2 tbsp. pesto sauce Black pepper ½ pound fresh Kale, roughly chopped

Put all of the ingredients in a slow cooker except the last one. Top with handfuls of kale and stuff the slow cooker with it. If you can't fit it all in at once, let the first batch cook first and add some more kale. Cook for 3or 4 hours on medium until summer squash become soft. Scrape the sides and serve.

Notes:

22. Slow-cooked Endives and Brussel Sprouts

INGREDIENTS (4 Servings)

1 ½ pounds brussel sprouts ½ onion, thinly sliced ¼ cup vegetable stock 1 tbsp. extra virgin olive oil Black pepper ½ pound fresh endives, roughly chopped

DIRECTIONS (20 minutes)

Put all of the ingredients in a slow cooker except the last one. Top with handfuls of endives and stuff the slow cooker with it. If you can't fit it all in at once, let the first batch cook first and add some more endives. Cook for 3 hours on medium until brussel sprouts become soft. Scrape the sides and serve.

Notes:

23. Buttery Swiss Chard and Turnips

INGREDIENTS (4 Servings)

1 ½ pounds turnips, peeled and cut into 1-inch chunks ½ onion, thinly sliced ¼ cup vegetable stock 4 tbsp. vegan butter or margarine 2 tbsp. lime juice 3 cloves garlic, minced Black pepper ½ pound fresh swiss chard, roughly chopped

DIRECTIONS (20 minutes)

Put all of the ingredients in a slow cooker except the last one. Top with handfuls of swiss chard and stuff the slow cooker with it. If you can't fit it all in at once, let the first batch cook first and add some more swiss chard. Cook for 3or 4 hours on medium until turnips become soft. Scrape the sides and serve.

Notes:

24. Slow Cooked Chinese Style Choy Sum & Carrots

1 ½ pounds carrots, peeled and cut into 1-inch chunks ½ onion, thinly sliced ¼ cup vegetable stock 1 tbsp. sesame oil 2 tbsp. hoi sin sauce Black pepper ½ pound choy sum, roughly chopped

Put all of the ingredients in a slow cooker except the last one. Top with handfuls of choy sum and stuff the slow cooker with it. If you can't fit it all in at once, let the first batch cook first and add some more choy sum. Cook for 3or 4 hours on medium until carrots become soft. Scrape the sides and serve.

Notes:

25. Slow Cooked Micro greens and Potatoes

1 ½ pounds potatoes, peeled and cut into 1-inch chunks ½ onion, thinly sliced ¼ cup vegetable stock 2 tbsp. extra virgin olive oil 1 tsp. annatto seeds 1 tsp. cumin 1 tsp. lime juice Black pepper ½ pound fresh Micro greens, roughly chopped

Put all of the ingredients in a slow cooker except the last one. Top with handfuls of micro greens and stuff the slow cooker with it. If you can't fit it all in at once, let the first batch cook first and add some more micro greens. Cook for 3or 4 hours on medium until potatoes become soft. Scrape the sides and serve.

Notes:

26. Slow Cooked Red Cabbage and Potatoes

1 ½ pounds potatoes, peeled and cut into 1-inch chunks ½ onion, thinly sliced ¼ cup vegetable stock 1 tbsp. extra virgin olive oil Black pepper ½ pound fresh Red cabbage, roughly chopped

DIRECTIONS (20 minutes)

Put all of the ingredients in a slow cooker except the last one. Top with handfuls of red cabbage and stuff the slow cooker with it. If you can't fit it all in at once, let the first batch cook first and add some more red cabbage. Cook for 3or 4 hours on medium until potatoes become soft. Scrape the sides and serve.

Notes:

27. Slow Cooked Choy Sum in Yellow Bean Sauce

1 ½ pounds turnips, peeled and cut into 1-inch chunks ½ onion, thinly sliced ¼ cup vegetable stock 1 tbsp. sesame seed oil 2 tbsp. chopped green onion, minced 4 tbsp. garlic, finely minced 2 tbsp. Chinese yellow bean sauce Black pepper ½ pound fresh choy sum, roughly chopped

DIRECTIONS (20 minutes)

Put all of the ingredients in a slow cooker except the last one. Top with handfuls of choy sum and stuff the slow cooker with it. If you can't fit it all in at once, let the first batch cook first and add some more choy sum. Cook for 3or 4 hours on medium until turnips become soft. Scrape the sides and serve.

Notes:

28. Slow Cooked Watercress and Chanterelle Mushrooms

INGREDIENTS (4 Servings)

1 ½ pounds chanterelle mushrooms ½ onion, thinly sliced ¼ cup vegetable stock 1 tbsp. extra virgin olive oil Rainbow peppercorns ½ pound fresh watercress, roughly chopped

DIRECTIONS (20 minutes)

Put all of the ingredients in a slow cooker except the last one. Top with handfuls of watercress and stuff the slow cooker with it. If you can't fit it all in at once, let the first batch cook first and add some more watercress Cook for 3or 4 hours on medium until mushrooms become soft. Scrape the sides and serve.

Notes:

29. Slow-cooked Porcini Mushrooms and Watercress

1 ½ pounds porcini mushrooms ½ onion, thinly sliced ¼ cup vegetable stock 1 tbsp. canola oil 2 tbsp. minced garlic Black pepper ½ pound fresh watercress, roughly chopped

Put all of the ingredients in a slow cooker except the last one. Top with handfuls of watercress and stuff the slow cooker with it. If you can't fit it all in at once, let the first batch cook first and add some more watercress. Cook for 3or 4 hours on medium until mushrooms become soft. Scrape the sides and serve.

Notes:

30. Slow Cooked Shitake Mushroom and Spinach in Hoi sin Sauce

INGREDIENTS (4 Servings)

1 pound shitake mushrooms, coarsely chopped ½ onion, thinly sliced ¼ cup vegetable stock 1 tbsp. sesame oil 2 tbsp. hoi sin sauce Black pepper ½ pound fresh spinach, roughly chopped

DIRECTIONS (20 minutes)

Put all of the ingredients in a slow cooker except the last one. Top with handfuls of spinach and stuff the slow cooker with it. If you can't fit it all in at once, let the first batch cook first and add some more spinach. Cook for 3or 4 hours on medium until mushrooms become soft. Scrape the sides and serve.

Notes:

31. Slow Cooked Curried Choy Sum & Button Mushrooms

1 ½ pounds button mushrooms ½ onion, thinly sliced ¼ cup vegetable stock 1 tbsp. extra virgin olive oil 1 tbsp. curry powder Black pepper ½ pound fresh choy sum, roughly chopped

Put all of the ingredients in a slow cooker except the last one. Top with handfuls of choy sum and stuff the slow cooker with it. If you can't fit it all in at once, let the first batch cook first and add some more choy sum. Cook for 3or 4 hours on medium until mushrooms become soft. Scrape the sides and serve.

Notes:

32. Slow cooked Collard Greens & Portobello Mushrooms

INGREDIENTS (4 Servings)

1 ½ pounds Portobello mushrooms ½ onion, thinly sliced ¼ cup vegetable stock 1 tbsp. extra virgin olive oil 2 tbsp. pesto sauce Black pepper ½ pound fresh collard greens, roughly chopped

DIRECTIONS (20 minutes)

Put all of the ingredients in a slow cooker except the last one. Top with handfuls of collard greens and stuff the slow cooker with it. If you can't fit it all in at once, let the first batch cook first and add some more collard greens. Cook for 3or 4 hours on medium until mushrooms become soft. Scrape the sides and serve.

Notes:

33. Slow cooked Endives and Porcini Mushrooms

INGREDIENTS (4 Servings)

1 ½ pounds porcini mushrooms ½ onion, thinly sliced ¼ cup vegetable stock 1 tbsp. extra virgin olive oil 2 tbsp. pesto sauce 1 tsp. Italian seasoning Black pepper ½ pound fresh endives, roughly chopped

DIRECTIONS (20 minutes)

Put all of the ingredients in a slow cooker except the last one. Top with handfuls of endives and stuff the slow cooker with it. If you can't fit it all in at once, let the first batch cook first and add some more endives. Cook for 3 or 4 hours on medium until mushrooms become soft. Scrape the sides and serve.

Notes:

34. Slow Cooked Kale and Button Mushrooms

1 ½ pounds button mushrooms ½ onion, thinly sliced ¼ cup vegetable stock 1 tbsp. extra virgin olive oil 1 tsp. cumin 1 tsp. annatto seeds 1 tsp. olives Black pepper ½ pound fresh Kale, roughly chopped

DIRECTIONS (20 minutes)

Put all of the ingredients in a slow cooker except the last one. Top with handfuls of Kale and stuff the slow cooker with it. If you can't fit it all in at once, let the first batch cook first and add some more Kale. Cook for 3or 4 hours on medium until mushrooms become soft. Scrape the sides and serve.

Notes:

35. Slow Cooked Romaine Lettuce and Chanterelle Mushrooms

1 ½ pounds chanterelle mushrooms ½ onion, thinly sliced ¼ cup vegetable stock 1 tbsp. extra virgin olive oil 1 tsp. garlic powder 1 tsp. onion powder Black pepper ½ pound fresh romaine lettuce, roughly chopped

Put all of the ingredients in a slow cooker except the last one. Top with handfuls of romaine lettuce and stuff the slow cooker with it. If you can't fit it all in at once, let the first batch cook first and add some more romaine lettuce. Cook for 3or 4 hours on medium until mushrooms become soft. Scrape the sides and serve

Notes:

36. Slow Cooked Micro Greens in Chimichurri Sauce

1 ½ pounds shitake mushrooms, sliced ½ onion, thinly sliced ¼ cup vegetable stock 1 tbsp. extra virgin olive oil 2 tbsp. chimichuri sauce Black pepper ½ pound fresh microgreens, roughly chopped

Put all of the ingredients in a slow cooker except the last one. Top with handfuls of microgreens and stuff the slow cooker with it. If you can't fit it all in at once, let the first batch cook first and add some more microgreens. Cook for 3or 4 hours on medium until mushrooms become soft. Scrape the sides and serve.

Notes:

37. Endives and Oyster Mushroom in Chimichurri Sauce

1 ½ pounds oyster mushrooms ½ onion, thinly sliced ¼ cup vegetable stock 2 tbsp. extra virgin olive oil 4 tbsp. chimichurri sauce Black pepper ½ pound endives, roughly chopped

Put all of the ingredients in a slow cooker except the last one. Top with handfuls of endives and stuff the slow cooker with it. If you can't fit it all in at once, let the first batch cook first and add some more endives. Cook for 3or 4 hours on medium until mushrooms become soft. Scrape the sides and serve.

Notes:

38. Triple Berry Jam

12 oz. blueberries, pureed 12 oz. strawberries, pureed 12 oz. raspberries, pureed 1 cup honey 2 teaspoons cinnamon 1/4 teaspoon ground ginger

Zest of 1 lemon Cook the blueberries on low for an hour. Stir after an hour and cook for another 4 hours. Add the spices, honey and zest. Remove the lid and cook for another hour. Place all of the ingredients in a blender and puree until smooth and store in a mason jar or container. Refrigerate.

Notes:

39. Spicy Slow Cooked Vegetarian Tacos Main

INGREDIENTS (4 Servings)

30 ounces red beans 2 cans of 15 ounces each, drained of water 1 cup corn canned, frozen or fresh 3 ounces chipotle pepper in adobo sauce, chopped 6 ounces tomato paste 1 can 3/4 cup Chili Sauce 2 tsp.

DIRECTIONS (20 minutes)

Unsweetened Cocoa Powder 1 teaspoon Ground Cumin 1/4 teaspoon Ground Cinnamon Ingredients for Garnishing and Serving 8 taco shells hard white corn or your favorite, hard or soft favorite toppings such as lettuce, avocado, lime Sea salt Place all of the main ingredients in a slow cooker Cook on low heat 3 1/2 hours or on high heat for 2 hours. Spread the ingredients on the taco shells, hard or soft. Top with lettuce. Add the tomatoes, avocado, and lime. Serve with beans and rice.

Notes:

40. Baked Chickpeas and Broccoli

cooking spray 1 tablespoon olive oil 4 cloves garlic, minced 1/2 teaspoon sea salt 1/4 teaspoon ground white pepper 3 cups sliced broccoli 2 ½ cups cherry tomatoes 1 (15 ounce) can chick peas, drained 1 small lime, cut into wedges 1 tablespoon chopped fresh cilantro

Preheat your oven to 450 degrees F. Line a baking pan with aluminum foil and grease with oil. Mix the olive oil, garlic, salt, and pepper thoroughly in a bowl. Add the broccoli, tomatoes, and garbanzo beans and combine until well coated. Spread out in the baking pan. Add the lime wedges. Bake in the oven until vegetables are caramelized, for about 25 minutes. Remove lime and top with cilantro.

Notes:

41. Baked Carrots and Red Beets

2 cups mini cabbages, trimmed 1 cup large Sweet potato chunks
1 cup large carrot chunks 1 cup cauliflower florets 1 cup cubed
red beets 1/2 cup shallot chunks 2 tablespoons extra virgin olive
oil Sea salt Ground black pepper to taste

Preheat your oven to 425 degrees F. Set the rack to the second-
lowest level part of the oven. Submerge the Brussels sprouts in
salted water and let it soak for 15 minutes Drain the Brussels
sprouts. Combine the potatoes, carrots, cauliflower, beets, shallot,
olive oil, salt, and pepper in a bowl. Layer the vegetables in a
single layer onto a baking sheet. Roast in the oven until
caramelized for about 45 minutes.

Notes:

42. Baked Mini Cabbage in Balsamic Glaze

1 (16 ounce) package fresh mini cabbage 1 small white onion, thinly sliced 5 tablespoons olive oil, divided 1/4 teaspoon sea salt 1/4 teaspoon freshly ground black pepper 1 shallot, chopped 1/4 cup balsamic vinegar 1 teaspoon chopped dried rosemary

DIRECTIONS (20 minutes)

Preheat your oven to 425 degrees F. Mix the mini cabbage and onion thoroughly in a bowl. Add 4 tablespoons olive oil Season with salt, and pepper Spread the cabbage on a pan. Bake in the oven until mini cabbage and onion become tender for about 28 minutes. Heat 2 tablespoons olive oil in a pan over medium-high heat. Sauté shallot until tender for about 4 minutes. Add balsamic vinegar and cook until reduced for about 5 minutes. Add the rosemary into the glaze and pour over the vegetables.

Notes:

43. Vegetarian Taco

1 tablespoon extra virgin olive oil 1 red onion, diced 2 cloves garlic, minced 2 pcs. jalapeno, chopped 2 (14.5 ounce) cans lima beans, rinsed, drained, and mashed 2 tablespoons yellow cornmeal Seasoning Ingredients 1 1/2 tablespoons cumin 1 teaspoon Spanish paprika 1 teaspoon cayenne pepper 1 teaspoon chili powder 1 cup salsa

Heat olive oil over medium heat. Add the onion, garlic, and jalapeno pepper and sauté until tender. Add the mashed beans. Add the cornmeal. Add seasoning ingredients. Cover and cook for 5 minutes.

Notes:

44. Spicy Curried Lima Beans

4 potatoes, peeled and cubed 2 tablespoons olive oil 1 yellow onion, diced 6 cloves garlic, minced 1 (14.5 ounce) can diced tomatoes 1 (15 ounce) can lima beans , rinsed and drained 1 (15 ounce) can peas, drained 1 (14 ounce) can coconut milk Seasoning Ingredients 2 teaspoons ground cumin 1 1/2 teaspoons cayenne pepper 1 tbsp. and 1 teaspoon curry powder 1 tbsp. and 1 teaspoon garam masala 1 (1 inch) piece fresh ginger root, peeled and minced 2 teaspoons sea salt

DIRECTIONS (20 minutes)

Submerge the potatoes in salted water. Boil over high heat and reduce heat to medium-low. Cover and let it simmer until tender, for about 15 minutes. Drain let it dry for a minute and a half. Heat the olive oil in a skillet over medium heat. Add the onion and garlic; cook and stir until the onion turns translucent for about 5 minutes. Add the seasoning ingredients. Cook for 2 minutes more. Stir in the tomatoes, beans, peas, and potatoes. Add the coconut milk, and simmer for 8 minutes.

Notes:

45. Steamed Broccoli

INGREDIENTS (4 Servings)

20 pcs. broccoli florets, preferably blanched   1 teaspoon sesame seed oil 1/4 teaspoon sea salt 3 cups water

DIRECTIONS (20 minutes)

Place water in the bottom half of a steamer pan set. Add salt and oil, and bring to a boil. Place the vegetable in the top half of the steamer pan set. Steam for 5 to 10 minutes depending on the thickness of the vegetable, or until vegetable becomes tender.

Notes:

46. Steamed Cauliflower

20 pcs. cauliflower florets, rinsed and drained 1 teaspoon canola oil 1/4 teaspoon sea salt 3 cups water Place water in the bottom half of a steamer pan set. Add salt and oil, and bring to a boil.

DIRECTIONS (20 minutes)

Place the vegetable in the top half of the steamer pan set. Steam for 5 to 10 minutes depending on the thickness of the vegetable, or until vegetable becomes tender.

Notes:

47. Steamed Choy Sum

1 bunch choy sum 1 teaspoon sesame oil 1/4 teaspoon sea salt 3 cups water Place water in the bottom half of a steamer pan set. Add salt and oil, and bring to a boil.

Place the vegetable in the top half of the steamer pan set. Steam for 5 to 10 minutes depending on the thickness of the vegetable, or until vegetable becomes tender.

Notes:

48. Stir Fried Sweet Potatoes

1 onion, chopped 1/4 cup extra virgin olive oil 1 pound sweet potatoes, peeled and cubed 1 teaspoon sea salt Spice Mix 1/2 teaspoon cayenne pepper 1/4 teaspoon ground turmeric 1/4 teaspoon ground cumin 2 tomatoes, chopped

DIRECTIONS (20 minutes)

Sauté and brown the onion in oil in a pan. Add the sea salt, cayenne, turmeric and cumin. Stir in the potatoes and cook while stirring frequently for 10 min. Stir in the tomatoes and cover Cook until potatoes become soft, for about 11 minutes.

Notes:

49. Simple Red Bean and Jalapeno Burrito

2 (10 inch) flour tortillas 2 tablespoons olive oil 1 small red onion, chopped 1/2 green bell pepper, chopped 2 teaspoon minced garlic 1 (15 ounce) can red beans, rinsed and drained 1 teaspoon minced jalapeno peppers 3 ounces ricotta cheese 1/2 teaspoon sea salt 2 tablespoons chopped fresh cilantro Wrap tortillas in a foil Bake them in a preheated 350 degree oven for 15 minutes.

DIRECTIONS (20 minutes)

Heat oil in a pan over medium heat. Place red onion, bell pepper, garlic and jalapenos in a pan. Cook for 2 minutes while stirring occasionally. Pour the beans into the pan and cook for 3 minutes while constantly stirring. Cut dairy free cream cheese into cubes and add to the pan with salt. Cook for 2 minutes while stirring. Add cilantro into this mixture. Spoon this evenly on the center of every warmed tortilla and roll the tortillas up.

Notes:

50. Ramen and Tofu Stir Fry with Sweet and Sour Sauce

1 (3.5 ounce) package ramen noodles (such as Nissin(R) Top Ramen) 3 tablespoons sesame seed oil 1 slice firm tofu, cubed 1/2 thai bird chillies, chopped 1/4 small red onion, chopped 1/3 cup plum sauce 1/3 cup sweet and sour sauce

Boil a pot of lightly salted water. Cook the noodles in boiling water and stir occasionally, until noodles are tender but still firm to the bite, 2 to 3 minutes. Drain the noodles. Heat oil in a pan over high heat. Place the tofu on one side of the pan. Place the chilies and the red onion on the other side of the pan. Cook a tofu until browned on all sides for 2 minutes. Cook and stir onion and pepper until browned, 2 minutes. Stir in the noodles into the pan Combine the noodles, tofu, onion, and pepper. Pour the plum sauce and sweet and sour sauce over the noodle. Sauté until well-combined for 3 minutes.

Notes:

51. Spicy Curried Purple Cabbage

INGREDIENTS (4 Servings)

3 tablespoons olive oil 2 dried red chili peppers, broken into pieces 2 tsp. skinned split black lentils (urad dal) 1 teaspoon split Bengal gram (chana dal) 1 teaspoon mustard seed 1 sprig fresh curry leaves 1 pinch asafoetida powder 4 green chili peppers, minced 1 head purple cabbage, finely chopped 1/4 cup frozen peas (optional) salt to taste 1/4 cup grated coconut

DIRECTIONS (20 minutes)

Heat the oil in pan on medium-high heat Fry the red peppers, lentils, Bengal gram, and mustard seed in the oil. When the lentils begin to brown, add the curry leaves and asafoetida powder and stir. Add the green chili peppers and cooking for a minute more. Combine the cabbage and peas into this mixture. Season with sea salt. Cook until the cabbage wilts, for about 10 minutes. Add the coconut to the mixture and cook for 2 minutes more.

Notes:

52. Pesto Zucchini Noodles

INGREDIENTS (4 Servings)

1 tablespoon extra virgin olive oil 4 small zucchini, cut into noodle-shape strands 1/2 cup drained and rinsed chickpeas 3 tablespoons pesto, salt and ground black pepper to taste 2 tablespoons parmesan cheese ¼ cup grated gouda cheese

DIRECTIONS (20 minutes)

Heat olive oil in a pan over medium heat Cook the zucchini until tender for around 8 minutes. Add the chickpeas and pesto to the zucchini. Lower the heat to medium-low. Cook until the chickpeas are warm and zucchini is coated for about 5 minutes Season with salt and pepper. Transfer zucchini to a bowl and top with vegan cheese.

Notes:

53. Simple Caramelized Carrots

3 tbsp olive (a vegan brand, such as Earth Balance) 4 carrots (sliced into ¼ inch thick slices 2 tbsp maple syrup

Heat the olive oil on low. Add the carrots Increase the heat to medium-high and add the honey. Let the carrots cook Stir frequently until soft.

Notes:

54. Cauliflower and Carrot Stir-fry Batter

1 tablespoon cornstarch 1 1/2 cloves garlic, crushed 1 teaspoons chopped fresh ginger root, divided Ingredients 1/4 cup olive oil, divided 1 small head cauliflower , cut into florets 1/2 cup snow peas 3/4 cup julienned carrots 1/2 cup halved green beans 2 tablespoons soy sauce 2 1/2 tablespoons water 1/4 cup chopped red onion 1/2 tablespoon sea salt 1 teaspoons chopped fresh ginger root

DIRECTIONS (20 minutes)

In a bowl, combine the batter ingredients and 2 tablespoons olive oil until cornstarch dissolves. Combine the broccoli, snow peas, carrots, and green beans, tossing to lightly coat. Heat remaining 2 tablespoons oil in a pan over medium heat. Cook vegetables for 2 minutes Add the soy sauce and water. Add the onion, salt, and remaining 1 teaspoon ginger. Cook until vegetables are tender but still crisp.

Notes:

55. Roasted Winter Squash

One 3-pound winter squash-peeled, seeded and cut into 1-inch dice 2 tablespoons extra-virgin olive oil 1 1/2 teaspoons ground cumin 1 teaspoon ground parsley 1/4 teaspoon cayenne pepper Kosher salt and freshly ground pepper

DIRECTIONS (20 minutes)

Preheat your oven to 425°. In a bowl, combine the squash with the olive oil, cumin, coriander and cayenne. Season with salt and pepper. Layer the squash on a baking pan Roast in your oven for about 40 minutes or until tender

Notes:

56. Baked Summer Squash and Red Bell Peppers

1 small summer squash, cubed 2 red bell peppers, seeded and diced 1 sweet potato, peeled and cubed 3 Yukon Gold potatoes, cubed 1 red onion, quartered 1 tablespoon chopped fresh thyme 2 tablespoons chopped fresh rosemary 1/4 cup extra virgin olive oil 2 tablespoons balsamic vinegar Sea salt Freshly ground black pepper

Preheat your oven to 475 degrees F. Combine the squash, red bell peppers, sweet potato, and potatoes thoroughly. Separate the red onion quarters and add them. Combine the thyme, rosemary, olive oil, vinegar, salt, and pepper. Toss this together with vegetables. Layer on a large roasting pan. Roast for 38 minutes in the oven, while stirring every 10 minutes, or until vegetables start to brown.

Notes:

57. Vegetarian Enchilada

1 Tbsp canola oil 1 1/4 cups chopped red onion (1 medium) 1 1/4 cups chopped green bell pepper (1 medium) 5 cloves garlic, minced 1 1/2 cups dry quinoa 2 1/4 cups vegetable stock 1 (14.5 oz) can tomatoes with green chilies, not drained 1 8 oz can tomato sauce 2 Tbsp. chili powder 1 1/2 tsp ground cumin Salt and freshly ground black pepper, to taste 1 (14.5 oz) can black beans, drained and rinsed 1 (14.5 oz) can pinto beans, drained and rinsed 1 1/2 cups frozen corn 1 1/2 cups gouda cheese , shredded Sea salt Black pepper Toppings: Diced avocados , diced Roma tomatoes, chopped cilantro, lime wedges, chopped green onions

DIRECTIONS (20 minutes)

Heat oil in a pan over medium. In this oiled pan, sauté onion and bell pepper for 3 minutes. Add in the garlic and sauté 30 seconds longer. Pour the contents of the pan into a slow cooker. Cover and cook on high for 3 hours Add the corn and beans. Combine well and top with vegan cheese. Cover and cook until for 13 minutes longer.

Notes: